50 STATES TO CELEBRATE

Celebrating
PENNSYLVANIA

Text copyright © 2015 by Jane Kurtz
Cover and interior illustrations copyright © 2015 by C. B. Canga
Country and state map illustrations copyright © 2015 by Jennifer Thermes

For information about permission to reproduce selections from this book,
write to Permissions, Houghton Mifflin Harcourt Publishing Company,
215 Park Avenue South, New York, New York 10003.

www.hmhco.com

The text of this book is set in Weidemann.
The display type is set in Bernard Gothic.
The illustrations are drawn with pencil and colored digitally.
The maps are pen and ink, and watercolor.

Photograph of white-tailed deer on page 32 © 2015 by Photodisc/Getty Images
Photograph of ruffled grouse on page 32 © 2015 by Good Photo/Alamy
Photograph of mountain laurel on page 32 © 2015 by Adrian Sherratt/Alamy

About the cover: The illustration on the cover is a tribute to Philadelphia's roots as a center for
carousel-making in the early 1900s. The Parx Liberty Carousel with the eagle can be found in
the city's historic Franklin Square.

Library of Congress Cataloging-in-Publication Data
Kurtz, Jane.
Celebrating Pennsylvania / Jane Kurtz, C. B. Canga.
p. cm. — (Green light readers level 3)
ISBN 978-0-544-41973-5 trade paper
ISBN 978-0-544-41972-8 paper over board
1. Pennsylvania—Juvenile literature. I. Canga, C. B., illustrator. II. Title.
F149.3K87 2015
974.8—dc23
2014023535

Manufactured in China
SCP 10 9 8 7 6 5 4 3 2 1
4500521297

Celebrating
PENNSYLVANIA

Written by **Jane Kurtz**
Illustrated by **C. B. Canga**

Green Light Readers
Houghton Mifflin Harcourt
Boston   New York

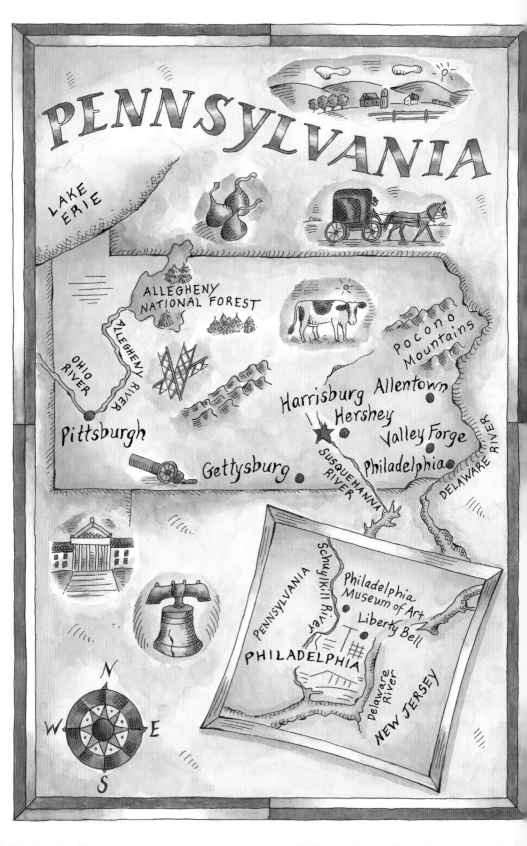

Hi, I'm Mr. Geo.

Here I am in Pennsylvania.

Its nickname is the Keystone State.

It played a key part

in the founding of our country.

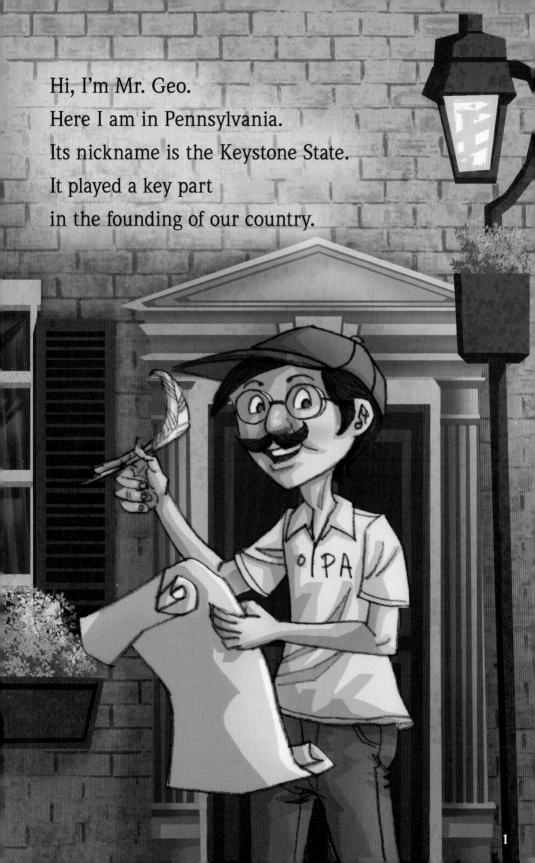

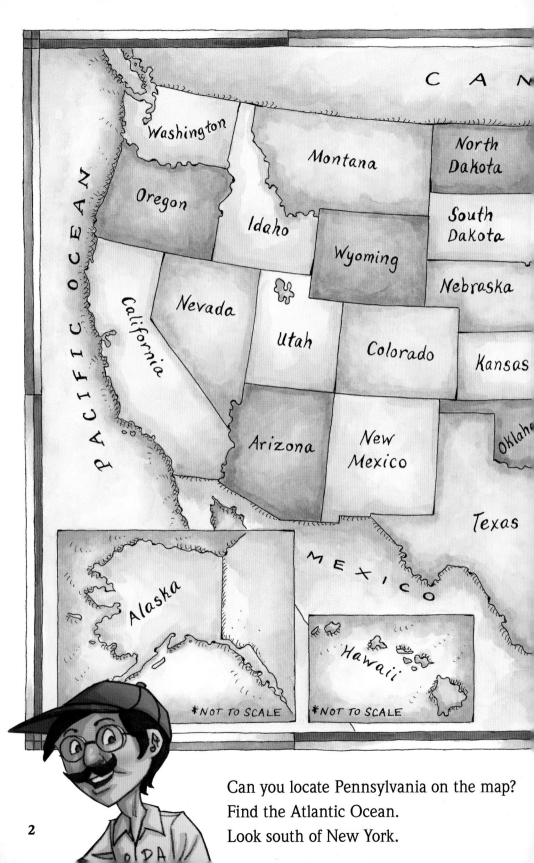

Can you locate Pennsylvania on the map?
Find the Atlantic Ocean.
Look south of New York.

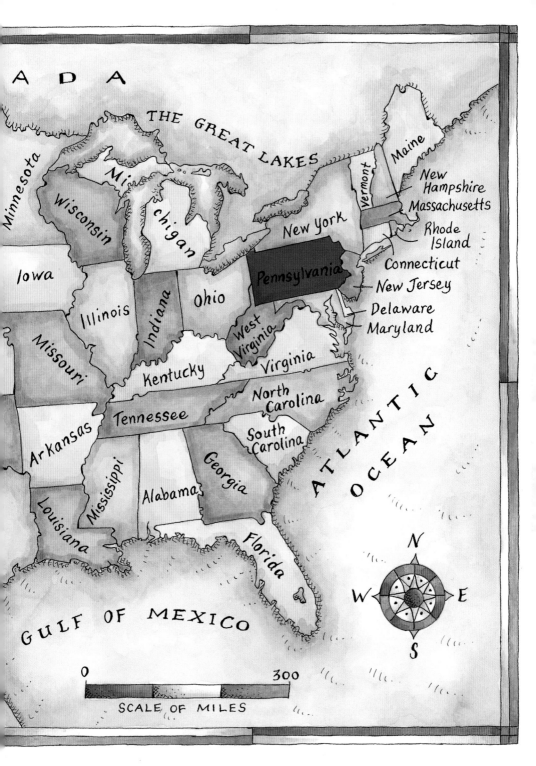

Now look north of West Virginia and Maryland.
Look east of Ohio and west of New Jersey.
The state in the middle is Pennsylvania.

Welcome to Philadelphia.

Hurrah! It's the Fourth of July.

This grand parade is ready to start.

Want to join me?

I'm leading the way through the Historic District,
all the way to Independence Hall.
I hope I don't miss a beat.

The Second **Continental Congress** approved the **Declaration of Independence** on July 4, 1776, at Independence Hall.

Hear ye! Hear ye!

That actor is about to recite famous lines from the **Declaration of Independence**.

It was an important document that announced the 13 colonies' freedom from British rule.

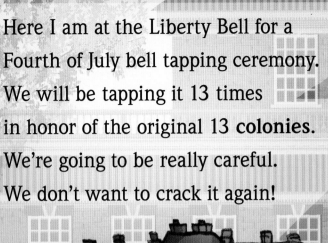

Here I am at the Liberty Bell for a
Fourth of July bell tapping ceremony.
We will be tapping it 13 times
in honor of the original 13 **colonies**.
We're going to be really careful.
We don't want to crack it again!

The Liberty Bell cracked in 1846 when it was
rung to celebrate George Washington's birthday.
No one knows why it cracked.

In Philadelphia's Historic District,
we can meet costumed characters from the past.
Today I shook hands with Benjamin Franklin.
He was one of our country's **Founding Fathers**.
He signed the Declaration of Independence.

Did you know?

In addition to being a **Founding Father,** Benjamin Franklin was an inventor, scientist, and writer.

Now I'm visiting Betsy Ross at her house.
She was a seamstress and **upholsterer**
who may have sewn the first American flag.
I'm not very good at sewing stars on this banner.
Ouch! I pricked my finger again!

The first flag had 13 stars, one star for each colony. Now the flag has 50 stars, one star for each state.

9

My nose led me to Reading Terminal Market.
This public marketplace has so many
delicious smells.

Pennsylvania is famous for some yummy foods!
Do you think I can eat this Philly cheesesteak
and still have room for a fresh-baked pretzel?

Did you know? You can learn how to hand-twist pretzels
at the country's first commercial pretzel
bakery in Lititz, Pennsylvania.

I'm stuffed! Time to get moving again!
This lovely parkway looks like the
perfect place to stroll.
It passes by grand museums, beautiful gardens,
a fancy fountain, and amazing statues.

At last! I'm at the Philadelphia Museum of Art.

I've always wanted to run up these steps.

I feel like a champion now!

The view from here is fantastic.

The award-winning movie *Rocky* about a boxer, was filmed in Philadelphia.

People in Pennsylvania love to root
for their favorite teams.
Wow, that Phillies player just stole home!
I have a plan to visit all the major-league parks.
Next on my list?
Pittsburgh, to watch the Pirates play.

Did you know?

Little League Baseball started in
Williamsport, Pennsylvania, in 1939.

If we visit Pennsylvania in winter,
we can cheer for football, basketball, and hockey.
In Philly, it's *Go Eagles! Go 76ers! Go Flyers!*
In Pittsburgh, it's *Go Steelers! Go Penguins!*

The Pittsburgh Steelers have won six Super
Bowls. That's more championships than any
other **NFL** team!

When I travel, I love to experience
different **cultures** and customs.
At the Museum of Indian Culture in Allentown,
we can see how the **Lenni Lenape** lived long ago.
Our guide showed us old ways of cooking food.
I can't wait to try this fire-roasted corn!

Did you know?

The Lenni Lenape used corn husks to make
mats, baskets, dolls, and moccasin liners.

Here in Lancaster County,
I'm learning about the ways of the Amish.
There is a quiet peacefulness
to roads without cars and homes with no TV.
Ah! *Clip-clop, clip-clop* is such a relaxing sound.

The Amish are also called Pennsylvania Dutch.

Many visitors come to Pennsylvania
to honor great American leaders.
George Washington spent a harsh winter
in **Valley Forge** during the **American Revolution.**
He trained soldiers for battle with the British.
I hope I remember my marching moves!

Before George Washington became the first
president of the United States, he was a general
in charge of the **Continental Army.**

In Gettysburg, I met a man who looked
like President Abraham Lincoln.
He was reciting Lincoln's most famous speech.
It honored soldiers who fought in the **Civil War**.
It stressed freedom and equality.

Lincoln delivered the **Gettysburg Address**
near the site of the **Battle of Gettysburg**
in 1863.

19

Rivers and railroads helped Pennsylvania grow.
They gave farmers and factory owners
a way to ship goods east, west, north, and south.

I came to Steamtown National Historic Site
to ride an old-fashioned train.
All aboard!

Did you know?

Pennsylvania's major waterways include
the Delaware, Susquehanna, Allegheny,
and Ohio Rivers, as well as Lake Erie.   **21**

Pennsylvania is full of farm animals and crops.

Thousands of cows.

Miles of cornfields.

Acres of apple trees and . . .

bunches and bunches of grapes!

Inventors have come up with some
amazing ideas in Pennsylvania.
Steel for railroad tracks.
Steamboats.
Chocolate candy bars.
Bubblegum.
Bottled ketchup.
My favorite? Crayons!

Did you know?

A pair of cousins, Edwin Binney and C. Harold Smith, started manufacturing the first Crayola boxed crayons in the early 1900s.

Forests cover much of Pennsylvania.
Here in the Pocono Mountains,
we can zip along, looking down at treetops.
I love the feeling of air in my hair.

Watching bald eagles is a popular activity
in the Poconos during the winter.

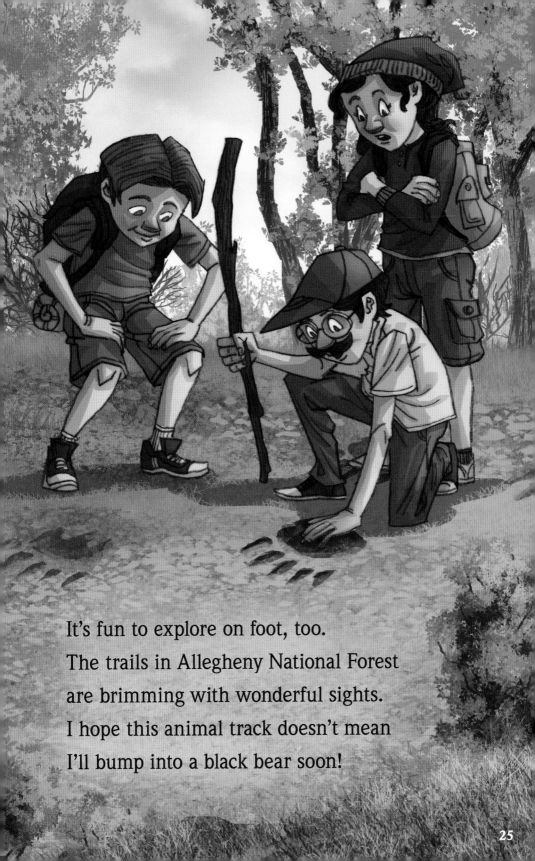

It's fun to explore on foot, too.
The trails in Allegheny National Forest
are brimming with wonderful sights.
I hope this animal track doesn't mean
I'll bump into a black bear soon!

Pennsylvania has many cities and towns.
Harrisburg, the state capital,
is home to the State Museum.
Have you met my friend William Penn?
He established the colony of Pennsylvania.

Did you know?

Pennsylvania was named after William Penn. It means "Penn's woodlands." (*Sylvan* means "full of trees, woods.")

Pittsburgh is a city where three rivers meet.
Over the years, it has been home to
many inventors, industrialists, and institutions.
Want to join me at the Children's Museum?
We can create our own inventions there!

Did you know?

The Carnegie Science Center has an exhibit that features robots used in movies, TV shows, factories, and space travel!

The sweetest city has to be Hershey.
This is where Milton Hershey built
his world-famous chocolate factory.
I saw how candy bars are made at Chocolate World.
I saw streetlights shaped like Hershey's Kisses
downtown.
But what I love most? The rides at Hershey Park!

Groundhog Day is a big day in
the small town of Punxsutawney.
That's when Phil comes out of his burrow
to predict whether spring will arrive late or early.

According to folklore, if a groundhog sees its
shadow on February 2, spring will arrive late
that year.

Pennsylvania has always been a state
bursting with big, bold ideas
and chances to have wonderful adventures.

Whether I see my shadow or not,
I predict that I will be back!
The Keystone State is one place where
I won't ever run out of sites to explore.

Fast Facts About Pennsylvania

Nickname: The Keystone State

State motto: Virtue, Liberty, Independence

State capital: Harrisburg

Other major cities: Philadelphia, Pittsburgh, Allentown, Erie, Reading, Scranton, Bethlehem, Lancaster

Year of statehood: 1787

State mammal: White-tailed deer

State bird: Ruffed grouse

State flower: Mountain laurel

State flag:

Population: Approximately 12.7 million, according to the 2013 census.

Fun fact: Hershey Park was originally built for people who worked at Milton Hershey's chocolate factory.

Dates in Pennsylvania History

1500: The Lenni Lenape people are living along the Delaware River.

1682: William Penn settles in the Philadelphia area and establishes Pennsylvania as an English colony.

1776: The Declaration of Independence is approved in Philadelphia.

1777: First national flag approved.

1777–78: George Washington and the Continental Army spend a difficult winter camped at Valley Forge during the American Revolution.

1787: The **U.S. Constitution** is written and approved in Philadelphia.

1790–1800: Philadelphia serves as the capital of the United States.

1846: The Liberty Bell cracks and cannot be repaired or rung again.

1850s: Coal mining, iron and steel manufacturing, and the railroad industry trigger a period of economic growth in Pennsylvania.

1863: The Battle of Gettysburg takes place during the Civil War; President Abraham Lincoln delivers the Gettysburg Address.

1865: The Civil War ends.

1947: Little League Baseball's first World Series is played in Pennsylvania.

2006: Historic Franklin Square in Philadelphia undergoes a makeover that includes a carousel, playground, and a restored water fountain.

2008: The Philadelphia Phillies win the World Series.

2009: The Pittsburgh Steelers win their sixth Super Bowl Championship; the Pittsburgh Penguins win the Stanley Cup.

Activities

1. **LOCATE** the six states that border Pennsylvania. Then, **SAY** each state's name out loud.

2. **DESIGN** a picture postcard for Pennsylvania. On the back, write a short message to a friend about what you drew.

3. **SHARE** two facts you learned about Pennsylvania with a family member or friend.

4. **PRETEND** you are a listening to your favorite radio station in Pennsylvania. The announcer is running a trivia contest. If you can answer these questions about Pennsylvania correctly, you will win the contest.

   a. **WHEN** was the Declaration of Independence approved?

   b. **HOW MANY** stars were on the first flag of the United States?

   c. **WHERE** did George Washington spend a harsh winter with soldiers?

   d. **WHO** delivered the Gettysburg Address?

5. **UNJUMBLE** these words that have something to do with Pennsylvania. Write your answers on a separate sheet of paper.

   a. **BLIYRET LEBL** (HINT: it used to ring)

   b. **REPZLTE** (HINT: a snack food)

   c. **DRRIAAOL** (HINT: train travel)

   d. **KLRAIFNN** (HINT: a Founding Father)

   FOR ANSWERS, SEE PAGE 36.

Glossary

American Revolution: the war that won the 13 American colonies freedom from British rule; it took place from 1775–83. (p. 18)

Battle of Gettysburg: a historic Civil War battle fought in southeastern Pennsylvania in July 1863 in which Confederate forces (the Southern states) were defeated by the Union forces (the Northern states). (p. 19)

Civil War: the war between the Northern states (the Union forces) and the Southern states (the Confederate forces) that helped end slavery in the United States. (p. 19)

colony: a settlement ruled by a different country. (p. 7)

Continental Army: the army that George Washington led to fight the British during the American Revolution. (p. 18)

Continental Congress: the name given to a meeting of leaders from each of the 13 colonies during the American Revolution; the First Continental Congress met in 1774; the Second Continental Congress met at various times from 1775–81. The Second Continental Congress approved the Declaration of Independence. (p. 5)

culture: the customs, beliefs, and ways of living shared by a group of people. (p. 16)

Declaration of Independence: a statement announcing that the 13 American colonies were independent from the country of Great Britain. (pp. 5 and 6)

Founding Fathers (of the United States): political leaders who helped establish the government of the United States. (p. 8)

Gettysburg Address: an important speech that President Abraham Lincoln gave to honor soldiers who died at the Battle of Gettysburg during the Civil War; it is considered one of the greatest speeches ever given; it established the Civil War as a war to end slavery. (p. 19)

Lenni Lenape: a Native American people who lived along the Delaware River; also called the Delaware. (p. 16)

NFL: The abbreviation for the National Football League. (p. 15)

upholsterer: a person who is in the business of professionally using fabric to pad and cover couches and chairs; upholsterers often also sew drapes and curtains. (p. 9)

U.S. Constitution: the United States' written plan and rules for government; our country's constitution includes the Bill of Rights and 27 amendments. (p. 33)

Valley Forge: the place in Pennsylvania where George Washington and his soldiers camped for a long and difficult winter during the American Revolution; they lacked food, clothing, shoes, and supplies. (p. 18)

Answers to activities on page 34:

1) Delaware, Maryland, New Jersey, New York, Ohio, and West Virginia; 2) Postcard designs will vary; 3) Answers will vary; 4a) July 4, 1776, 4b) Thirteen (13), 4c) Valley Forge, 4d) Abraham Lincoln; 5a) LIBERTY BELL, 5b) PRETZEL, 5c) RAILROAD, 5d) FRANKLIN.